OPTICAL ILLUSIONS

An Eye-Popping Extravaganza of Visual Tricks

Gianni A. Sarcone and
Marie-Jo Waeber

Dover Publications, Inc.
Mineola, New York

Bibliographical Note

Optical Illusions: An Eye-Popping Extravaganza of Visual Tricks is a new work, first published by Dover Publications, Inc., in 2014.

International Standard Book Number
ISBN-13: 978-0-486-49354-1
ISBN-10: 0-486-49354-7

Manufactured in the United States by Courier Corporation
49354701   2014
www.doverpublications.com

CONTENTS

INTRODUCTION

*"Reality is merely an illusion,
albeit a very persistent one."*
-- Albert Einstein

Dear Reader,

Everything you "see" depends strongly on the context and attention you give to it. The mind and the world you experience are inseparable, as it is your 3-pound brain that make the world meaningful. Seeing isn't some kind of direct perception of reality. Actually, *our bairns are cnostanlty itnerperting, correcting, and giving srtuctrue to the viusal ipnut form our eeys*[1]. If this were not the case, you would not see any colors (consider that all the beautiful colors you see don't really exist), and you would probably see the world upside-down! Moreover, you would notice in your visual field a very large dot, called the "blind spot," where the optical nerve enters the eye.

A Zen master said once: "If you pour water into a cup, water becomes the cup; if you fill a bottle with water, it becomes the bottle!" Likewise, the context shapes the appearance of the world surrounding you. **Your brains work by comparing information and stimuli**: contrasting colors, shapes, depth in a dynamic changing environment … that's why perception is relative and not absolute.

Detecting something is not necessarily simple: your senses may perceive a stimulus, but that doesn't mean that you are paying attention to it! There are a lot of things you miss or ignore in your everyday life, because your brain focuses only on what seems important in that particular moment of your life. Removing or neglecting information is often more useful, because it allows you to take action in a more accurate and rapid manner, and to enjoy life's benefits.

Though you can see less than 1% of the electromagnetic spectrum and hear less than 1% of the acoustic spectrum, under the right conditions you can see the flicker of a small candle up to 9 miles (15 km) away, and can hear a watch ticking 20 feet (6 meters) away!

---

[1]*Most probably your brains have automatically corrected the sentence to "actually, our brains are constantly interpreting, correcting, and giving structure to the visual input from our eyes." It's amazing, isn't it?*

However, **if economy of perception makes functional living and survival possible, it is also the cause of many optical illusions**. From prehistory to the present day, optical illusions have helped us to reflect upon the reality of what is seen and understand a little better some of the errors of perception we make. Over the years, scientists have been studying and utilizing optical illusions to gain insights into how our brains interpret information and build a representation of the surroundings.

Yet illusions can also be employed as inspiration or improvement tools. In fact, stepping outside your comfort zone and thinking in ways that are both creative and challenging to your visual perception is a kind of exercise that may increase your brain flexibility.

Research says that humans are programmed to enjoy surprise. So, I am not surprised that many people love optical illusions, because they always convey a sense of WONDER.

Dear reader, enjoy being deceived by the optical illusions and visual puzzles you will find along the way in this book, and don't be afraid to make a lot of mistakes, because they are just important stages on the road of knowledge.

About the Author

As an author, designer, and researcher in the field of visual perception and creative thinking, I like to combine art, psychology, cognitive sciences, and recreational logic to test people's ingenuity.

I have created or adapted most of the illusions contained in this book. Many were created and perfected during my workshops which are held for the benefit of children and adults alike (more information at:(**http://www.archimedes-lab.org/prospatelier.html**).

For me, imagination, inventiveness, and exploration are the cornerstones of a meaningful life. Each helps to stimulate our mind and assures us of a fulfilling day, every day. As an artist, I feel it is my task, as well as my pleasure, to entertain an audience with illusions that challenge the mind and bring a sense of WONDER.

This book is intended to communicate the latest discoveries in the field of visual perception in an entertaining way. I hope it will also prompt the curious to look beyond what seems obvious, to think and to see outside of the box!

Gianni A. Sarcone
Artist and visual perception researcher

SHAPES, DISTANCES & SIZES

Our brains often translate the physical image we perceive into an image which is more useful to our senses. But, as you will experience in this chapter, there is a sharp distinction between the "actual size" of an object, its apparent or relative size, and its imaginary size. Shape distortion and errors of size estimation have various causes, including the fact that we "think" in 3D even when we look at photos or drawings. Answers to this section begin on page 56.

A Question of Hands

Have a look at this special clock/watch. Can you guess which is the hour hand and which is the minute hand?

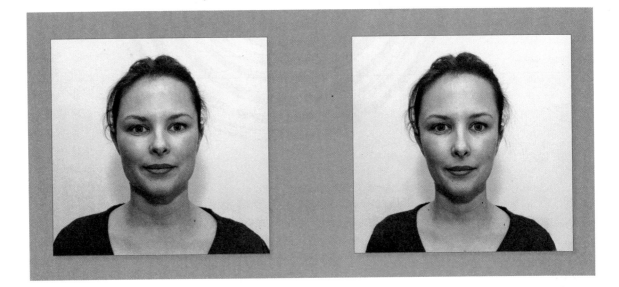

Hat Story

Which girl needs a bigger hat to fit her head?

Pointing Fingers

In your opinion, which forefinger points EXACTLY to the middle of the shape's height: A or B? Please explain what influenced your choice!

Puzzling Hubcaps

Take a careful look at the color lines across the two ellipses, which represent the hubcaps of the tractor. Which line is the longest: the blue line or the red one?

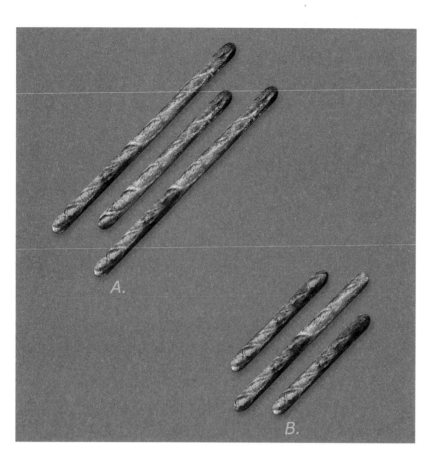

A.

B.

French Dilemma

Look carefully at the two appetizing sets of French baguettes in figures A and B. Are the middle-sized baguettes in each figure the same size? Or is the middle-sized baguette in A slightly longer than the one in B?

Hypnotic Disc

Observe the disc steadily. How many spirals do you perceive?

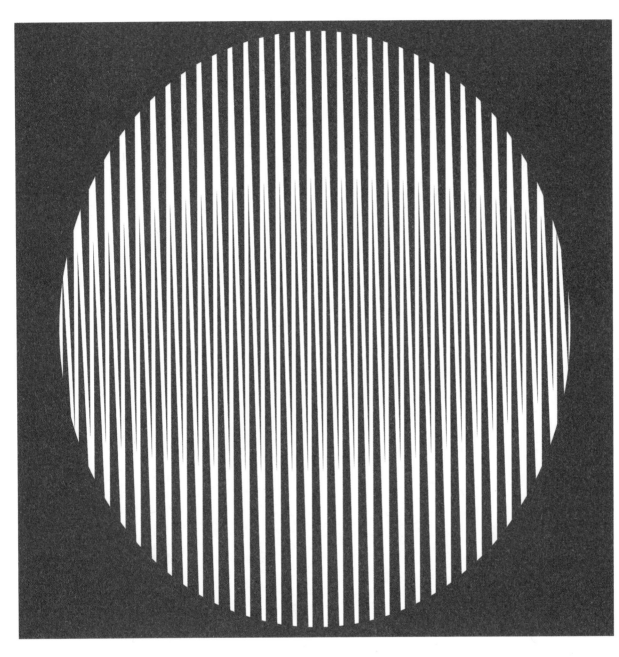

Boing Effect?

While staring at the picture, move your head to and away from it.
What happens?

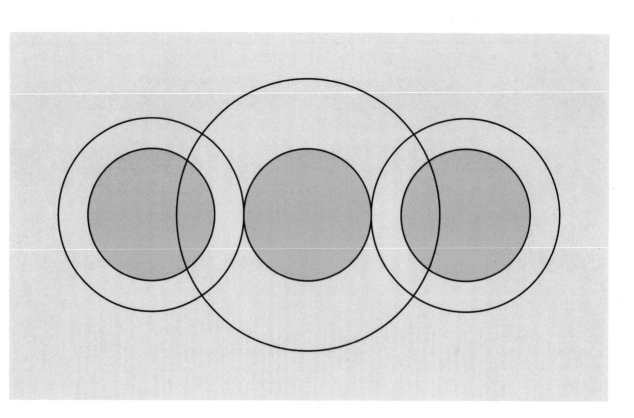

Puzzling Disks

Is the central pink disk smaller, larger, or equal to the other adjacent disks?

What Is It?

What kind of three-dimensional shape/object do you see?

Hovering Diamonds

Are the three floating concentric shapes skewed diamonds or perfect squares? Does the background vibrate?

Crowd of Young People

Describe accurately the people in this picture.

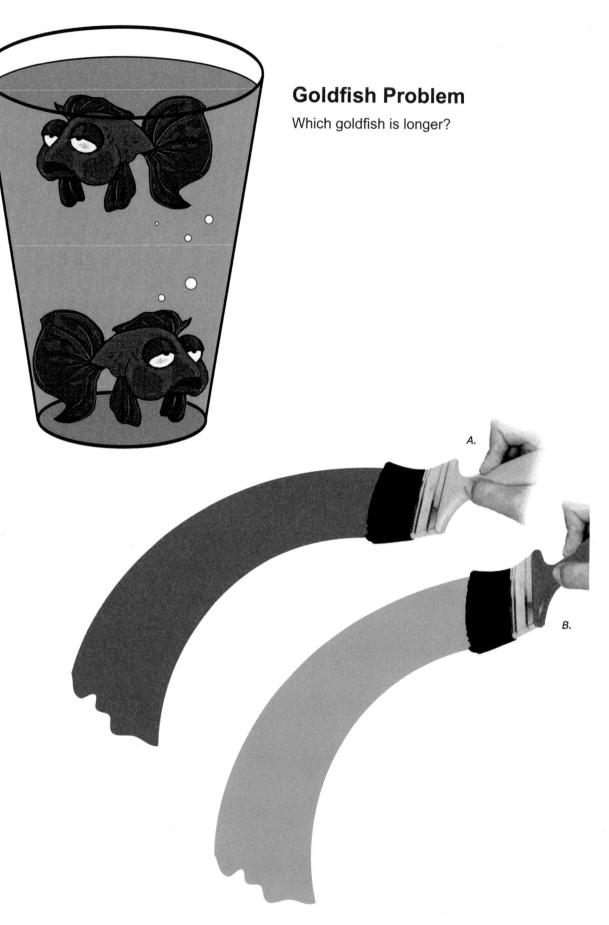

Goldfish Problem

Which goldfish is longer?

Brush Illusion

Which one of those two brushes in fig. A and B has painted the longest color stroke?

Roman Temple

Do the columns of this Roman temple converge (or diverge)?

The Puzzling Pearl Earring

Look carefully at the two books featuring on the cover the "Girl with a Pearl Earring" by Vermeer. Are the covers the same size? Do the pictures and the titles have exactly the same length and width?

How to Become a Giant…

The Palazzo Spada in Rome, Italy, contains a strange alcove where people seem to grow as they walk away down the corridor! How is this possible?

Question of Font

Which character is wider: the letter H or the W?

Fall

Does the picture suggest an autumnal impression of falling maple leaves?

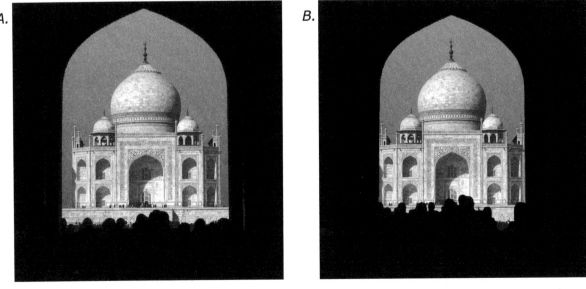

Taj Mahal Illusion

The Taj Mahal is a marble mausoleum located in India. Can you say in which picture it appears larger: in fig. A or in fig. B?

Moving Diamonds

Do the diamond-like shapes have wobbly corners? Are they moving?

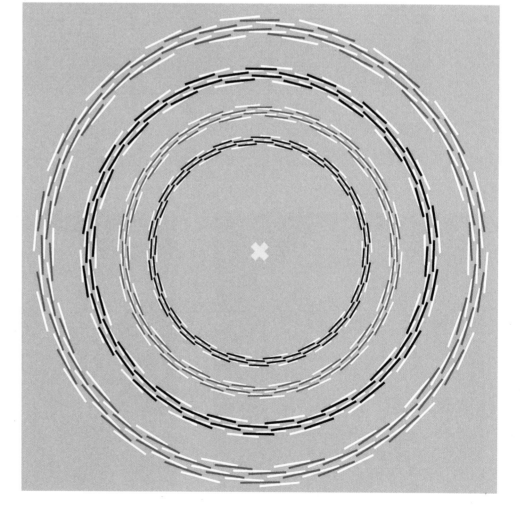

Rotation Arcs

Do the 4 rings share exactly the same center? What happens if you move your head away and toward the picture while staring at the central cross?

Parallel or Connvergent?

Do the vertical alignments of colored segments converge toward the top?

Women Diving

Are both divers the same size?

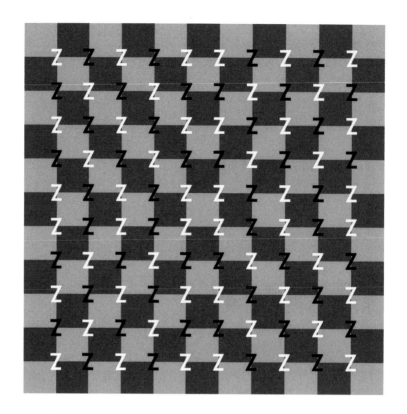

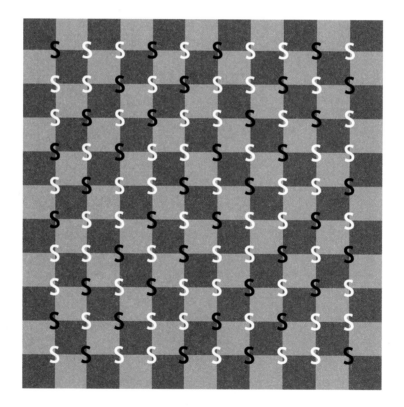

Distorted by Fonts?

As you can see, alternating black and white capital
letters have been distributed on a checkered surface.
Are the brown and blue squares distorted?

COLOR & SUBJECTIVE MOTION

We have a secret we wish to share with you… Color doesn't exist at all in nature! Color only starts to exist when your perception systems produce the impression of "color": light is perceived on the retina as a stimulus and is processed into a perception of color in your brains. So, when you look at a rainbow, you create it (to animals without cells sensible to color, the rainbow simply does not exist!).

As you will see in the following pages, colors and contrasts can also induce some interesting motion effects in our peripheral vision field. Answers to this section begin on page 60.

Befuddling Squares

Match the pair of blue squares that have the same hue and brightness:
A and C, or A and D, or B and C, or maybe B and D?

Unstable Triangles

Are the triangles surrounded by the purple Pacman-like shapes lighter or darker than the triangle-patterned background?

Does Everything Really move?

What happens when you move your eyes around the picture?

Kite Pattern

Can you guess which line of bright and dark green squares is most like the decorative pattern in the middle of the kite: A, B, or C?

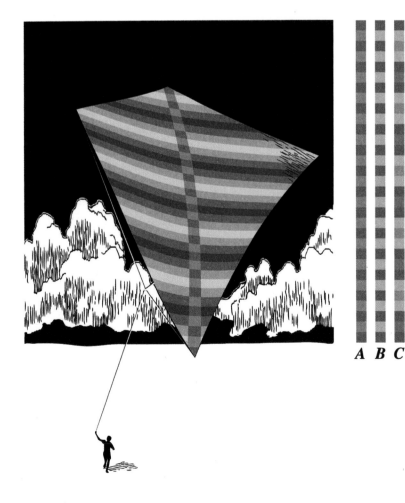

A B C

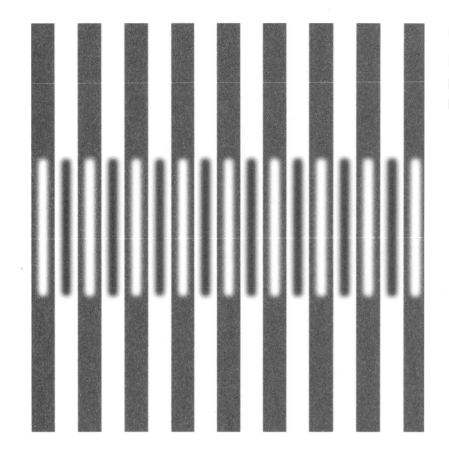

Op' Art Illusion

Do you notice something peculiar in this geometric pattern?

Magic Spirals?

Do you see spirals? Does the circular pattern expand or rotate?

Puzzling Color

What color are the tiny balls at the intersections of the Chinese symbols known as hexagrams? Some people say that they are yellow, others argue the spots are green instead. What is your own opinion?

Color Assimilation

Can you say if the color of the parallel grey bars is uniform?

Hypno-Discs

Slowly move your gaze around the picture. Do you notice anything strange?

Off-Color Apples

The colors in this drawing representing an arrangement of apples are not well balanced... Do you agree? Actually, the left side is reddish while the right side has too much green. Do you want to help the artist? Stare at the center cross of the red and green table for 20-30 seconds, and then look at the drawing again. Do you notice something special?

Blurry Faces

You can see in the upper picture a blurry face of a woman and another one sharp. Stare at the fixation star between these two faces for about 20-30 seconds. Then QUICKLY look at the fixation star of the lower picture. Do you notice something particular?

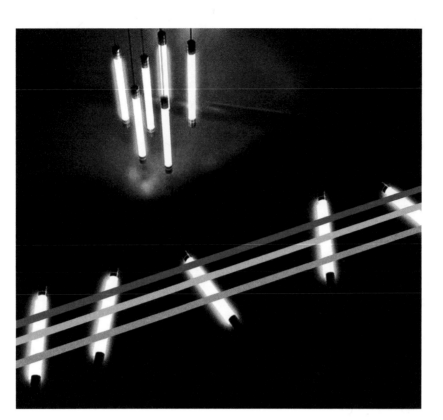

Neon Troubles

Is the color of the stripes crossing the neon even and uniform or are there dark smudges on them?

Vibrations

Is something in the picture vibrating?

Hypnosis

Just concentrate at the center of the pattern of concentric rings. Do you notice something particular?

Oriental Fan

Do the pleated surfaces of the fan have the same shade?

Unstable Beats

Is the heart beating, moving, or hovering over the back-ground?

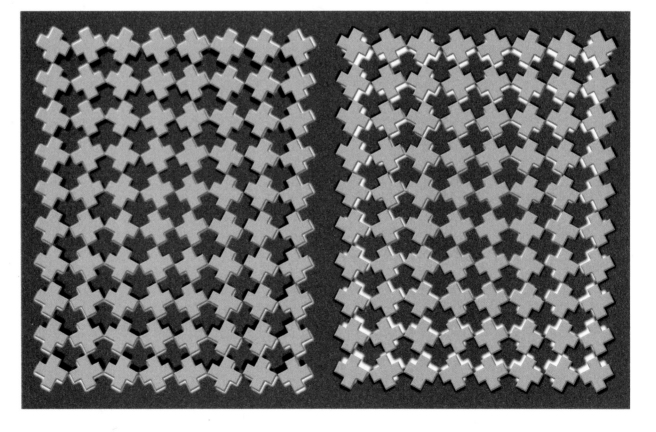

"Eppur Si Muove" (Galileo)

Look at this picture for a while. Don't you have the feeling that it is moving? Can you describe what exactly happens here?

Soccer Ball

As you see, the soccer ball is covered with hexagonal and pentagonal panels. Are the panels A and B of the ball exactly the same hue?

Mycenaean Painting

Observe carefully the painted wall of this antique Greek house: are the curled shapes of the same color and shade?

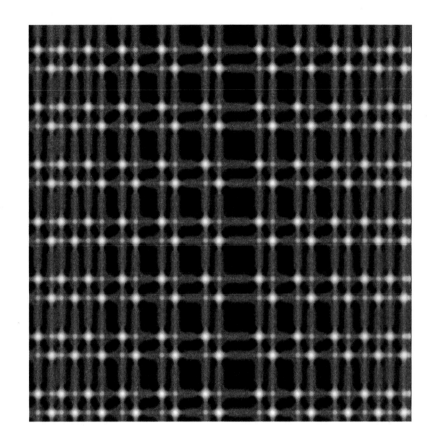

Ghost Dots?

Can you see the dark "ghost" blobs or black smudges at the intersections of the lines? Do they really exist?

Up and Down Flows

Is the picture still?

Neon Blue

It looks like a translucent blue twisting sheet lies over the electronic circuit. Do you agree?

Face of Wonder

Close one eye and focus your attention on the nose for about 20–30 seconds. Do you experience something peculiar?

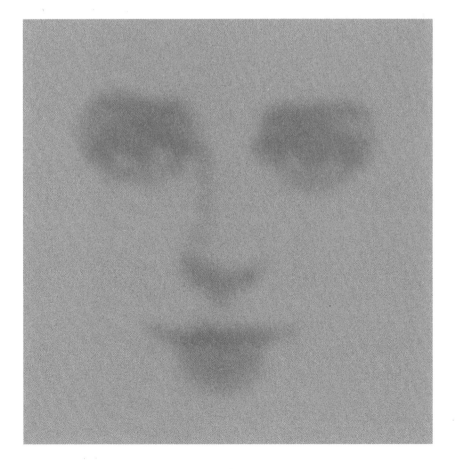

Pasta Still Life

Which color is the border of the plate – a, b, or c? Is the circular decorative line best represented by color 1, color 2 or color 3?

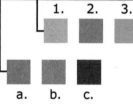

1.   2.   3.

a.   b.   c.

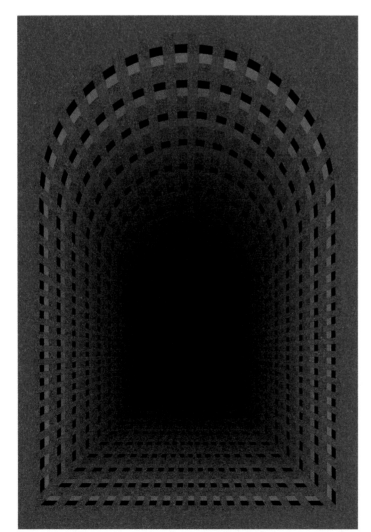

Tunnel Effect

What is there to worry about in this mysterious tunnel?

AMBIGUOUS & IMPOSSIBLE FIGURES

"Impossible figures" are objects that cannot exist according to the known laws of physics but have a description or representation suggesting, at first sight, that they can be constructed. Generally, when a portion of a depicted object conveys conflicting depth or position cues such as ahead/behind, front/back, inward/outward, above/below or top/bottom, there are chances that you are in presence of an impossible figure.

"Ambiguous figures" are pictures or objects that generally present the viewer with a choice of two or more interpretations, each of which may be valid. As you will learn in the following pages, the large family of ambiguous illusions includes figure-ground illusions, reversible figures and, composite figures. Answers to this section begin on page 65.

Elephant or Bull Delusion Illusion

The bull and the elephant, representing respectively Lord Shiva and Ganesh, are a recurrent motive in Hindu mythology as shown in this ceiling painting of the Sri Meenakshi temple in Madurai. Our question is whether the head portrayed belongs to an elephant or is it a bull's head instead? Or could it be both at the same time?

Brrr... Scary Night

Do you notice something strange in this scene with a mysterious woman holding a candelabrum?

Impossible Furniture

In this waiting room there are at least two impossible objects hidden among the retro furniture. Try to spot them! Are you able to perceive one of the plastic armchairs under two different perspectives?

Trumpet Player

What happens when the
trumpeter blows in the trumpet?

Lumberjack

How many trees can
be cut down in this
mysterious forest?

Mask of Love?

The picture shows a mask of a pensive person. But is it a woman or a man?

Hesitant Bookcase

Wall bookcase with 4 or 3 shelves?

Amazing Impossible Structure

Try to mentally guess which part is perspectively incorrect in the structure.

Enchanted Staircase

Starting from A and going directly to B, the jogging woman will climb the same number of steps whether she runs to the left or to the right. However, if she decides to go from A to B by crossing the bridge once, something strange happens. Can you guess what?

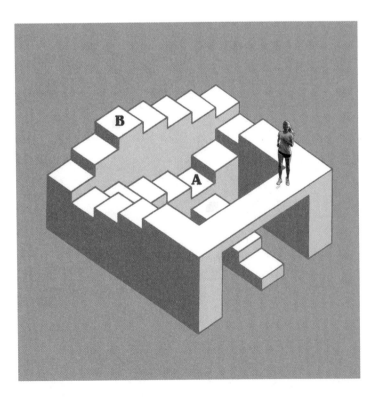

Gift Warp

How would I wrap this crate?
Any suggestions?

Polyvalent Bookshelf

What is wrong with this bookshelf?

Hallucinatory Staircase

What happens if you try to climb to the top of this mysterious staircase?

Annoying Urban Furniture

Can such an architectural structure exist?

Quadri-Dimensional room?

In this strange space-dimension the parquet floor appears to be also the ceiling of the room! How is this possible?

TESTS & EXPERIMENTS

Visual and intuitive puzzles test your concentration and your visual discrimination ability. This chapter will tell you much about the way you see and look at the world you live in. Answers to this section begin on page 68.

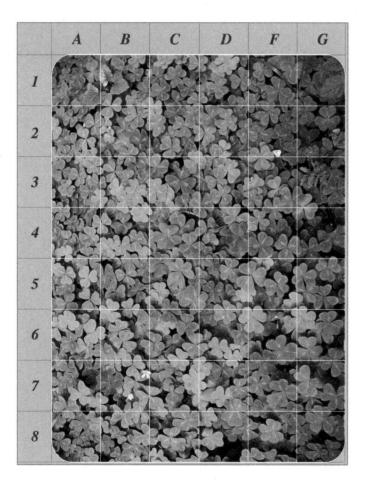

Spotting the Blind Spot

Close your right eye and hold this picture about 10–12 inches (25–30 cm) from your left eye. Look at the dot between the magician's eyes and slowly move the page forward and back until one heart on the playing card disappears. Why does this happens?

Honeymoon

Find 4 lovers in this nocturnal scene lit by a smiling moon.

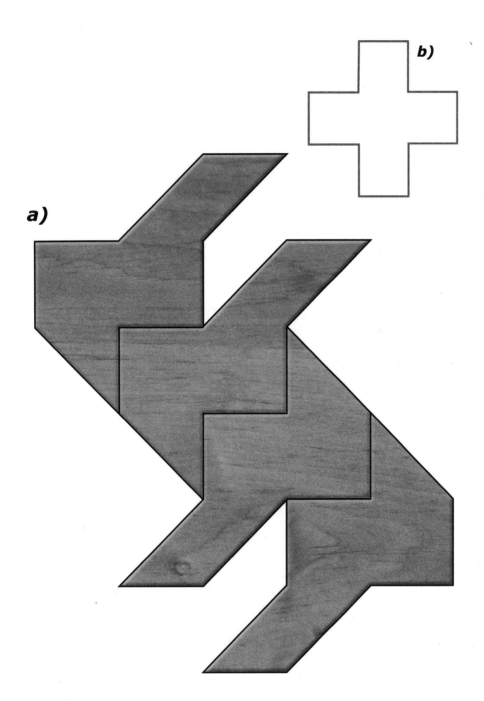

a)

b)

Broken Swiss Cross

Reproduce this 4-piece puzzle (fig. a) onto a piece of cardboard or Bristol paper and cut out its pieces. Your goal is to assemble those pieces into the shape of a cross as shown in fig. b. Will you be able to achieve this challenge? Believe us... it isn't so obvious!

Peaceful Scenery?

This silhouette represents a Japanese bonsai on a pedestal. Though this scene inspires calm, there is something irritating within the picture.

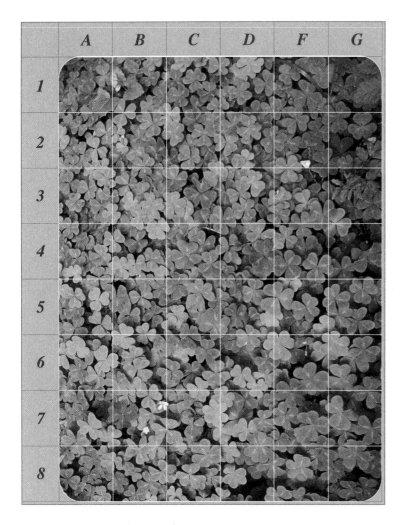

	A	B	C	D	F	G
1						
2						
3						
4						
5						
6						
7						
8						

St. Patrick Visual Puzzle

You get 5 minutes to find all 5 four-leaf lucky clovers!

Ambiguous Message

Can you believe that this nice girl sports a T-shirt with a hate message? No. Surely there's a hidden message somewhere in the picture. Can you spot it?

Wow effect

Place a rectangular beauty mirror right under your nose as shown in the picture and then try to walk around your room while looking in the mirror. What happens?

Crack the Message

Research says if you can read this you have a strong mind!

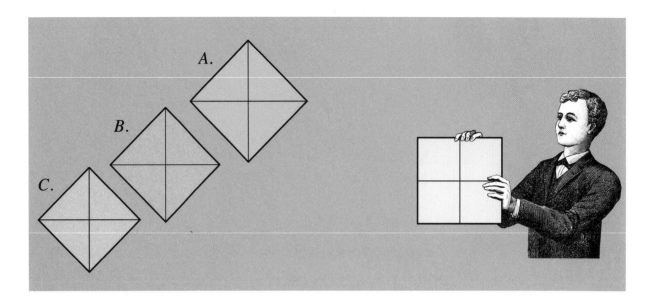

The Unsizable Square

Which diamond A, B or C has exactly the same size as the square held by the boy?

Mystery Comb

Can you guess who this comb belongs to?

Halloween Popcorn

How many spooky skulls can you spot in this bowl of popcorn?

Crack this Martian Sentence

Will you be able to read this sentence written in an unknown language?

Young Girl with Cat

What's wrong with this picture?

Hidden Zebras

Find the other three zebras within this picture.

Camouflaged?

Is the knife shown in the picture transparent?

Hidden Giraffe

Spot the other "giraffe" in this exotic old engraved landscape.

Pair of Oddness

There was a party but where is the bottle? Do you see another oddity?

Mysterious Reflection

How is this possible? Can you solve this visual puzzle?

Haunted House

Hmmm… Here is a haunted house, where is the ghost?

Incomplete Keyboard

This is a visual attention test. Does the typed sentence contain all the letters of the alphabet? If not, which one is missing?

> When I was in Uruguay, Mr John B. Hitchcock gave me a plywood box of quite a small size.

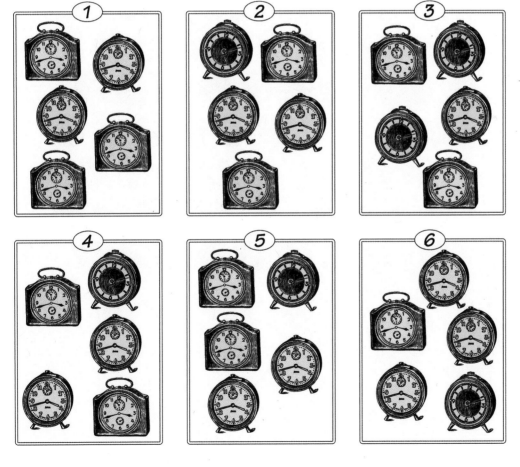

Batches

Which batch has to be eliminated to get the same number of each kind of clocks?

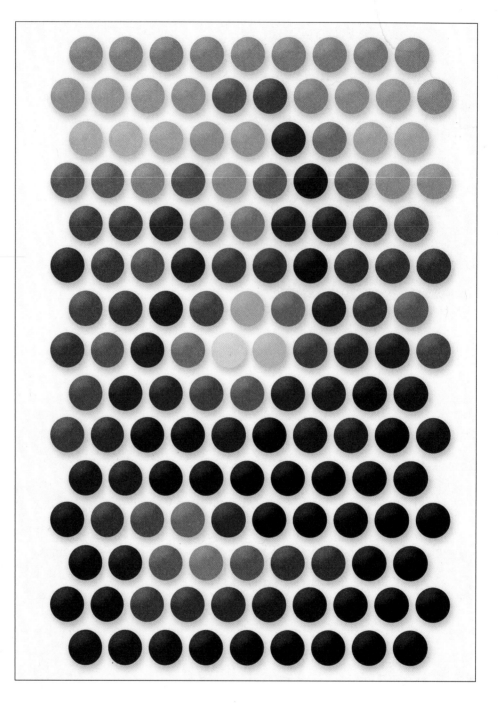

Hidden Portrait

Can you see a famous painting in this alignment of color marbles?

ANSWERS

Page 2

A Question of Hands

Answer: Most people answer that the vertical hand is the hour hand, because it looks shorter. However, both hands are the same length. If you don't believe it, measure the segments for yourself! This optical effect is related to the "Müller-Lyer illusion", where two segments of equal length do not seem the same when framed by angle brackets with the spikes towards the inside or the outside.
Well, why do the long (and thinner) hands of the clock always represent minutes? Because minutes have to be precise that is why the minute hands have to be long enough to touch the numbers or the signs around the dial.

Page 2

Hat Story

Answer: The girl on the left seems to have a broader head than the thin one. This impression is especially pronounced if you look at the face rather than the top of the head. Actually, both girls could wear a hat of exactly the same size because their forehead and top of the head are identical. We experience such illusions in our daily life: perception of a body feature is always influenced by other body parts.

Page 3

Pointing Fingers

Answer: Strangely enough, 80% of people are convinced that both fingers point at the same level (although the one on the right appears to be lower). Actually, only finger B points to middle of the shape's height, as demonstrated in the image below.

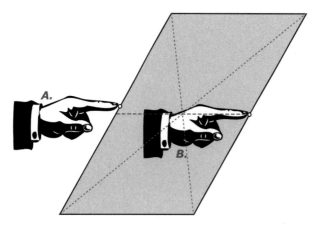

Page 3

Puzzling Hubcaps

Answer: Eighty to ninety per cent of people polled say the farthest red line is longer, but in fact it is shorter than the closest blue one. There are two factors that strongly influence the brain to arrive at the wrong answer: the context and the virtual distance of the hubcaps.

Page 4

French Dilemma

Answer: The middle-sized baguettes in A and B are both the same size. This illusion is related to the classic Müller-Lyer and Ebbinghaus illusions.

Page 4

Hypnotic Disc

Answer: You may see a continuous spiral. However, there isn't any spiral at all, because the main disc is composed only of a series of superposed yellow and black discs.

Page 5

Boing Effect?

Answer: The white curlicue-like shape behaves as a spring: when you approach your eyes it seems to expand, whereas when you move your head away, it appears to shrink! Strange, isn't it?

Page 6

Puzzling Disks

Answer: The three disks are exactly the same size. A disk appears slightly smaller when it is inscribed in a large circle, while it looks slightly larger when it is inscribed in a small circle.

Page 6

What Is It?

Answer: You may see a spotted spring-like device, but where are its contours? In fact, such a spring cannot exist, because it is formed by floating color disc and semicircles. This is a tridimensional variant of the subjective contour illusion called "Kanisza triangle."

Page 7

Hovering Diamonds

Answer: The three shapes that appear like slanted diamonds are in fact perfect squares. The tilting effect is based on Fraser's spiral illusion.

Page 7

Crowd of Young People

Answer: In the middle part of the picture, figures and ground are reversed! (For instance, the black background becomes legs and feet.) This kind of illusion is called "ambiguous figure/ground perceptual reversal".

Page 8

Goldfish Problem

Answer: Both are the same size. The bottom fish seems longer because of its proximity to the glass edge, making it appear tighter, and thus larger.

Page 8

Brush Illusion

Answer: Some of you may have answered the one which painted the orange stroke (fig. B)... This illusion is related to the "Jastrow illusion," an optical illusion discovered by the American psychologist Joseph Jastrow in 1889, involving two curvilinear shapes.
In this illustration, the two curved strokes are IDENTICAL, although the lower one appears to be larger. This cognitive illusion is mainly due to our prior assumption in perspective.

Page 9

Roman Temple

Answer: No, the columns of the temple are perfectly straight and parallel to each other. This interesting version of the Popple illusion demonstrates how vertical bars including an alignment of patterns adequately shifted can induce a tilt sensation.
The inscription under the pediment, "Mundus vult decipi, ergo decipiatur!" is a Latin phrase that means "The world wants to be deceived, so let it be deceived!"

Page 9

The Puzzling Pearl Earring

Answer: Though the cover of the book on the left appears longer and narrower, the books have an equal cover surface and both pictures and texts are identical in length and width. If you don't believe me, try and measure them for yourself. This neat illusion is a variant of the classic Roger Shepard's tabletop illusion, in which two identical quadrilaterals with different orientations to each other appear dissimilar in shape.

How to Become a Giant...

Answer: This effect called "forced perspective gallery" is due to an ingenious trick of the Renaissance architect, Francesco Borromini. He made the corridor, which is only about 10 meters (33 feet) long, look far longer by making both sides converge and by having the floor slightly leaning upward, reducing the height of the columns as they gradually recede from the entrance. You can see this in the sketches representing the bird's eye view in fig. a, and the lateral view in fig. b.

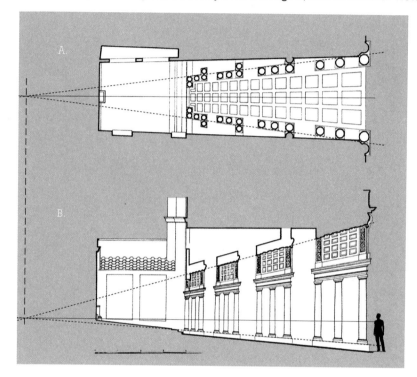

Question of Font

Answer: Though the H seems wider, both are of the same width.

Fall

Answer: Yes, the picture gives you an aerial view of leaves falling to the ground, although there are ONLY horizontal lines! (The thickness of the lines determines the depths of each leaf.) It is actually your brain that completes the gaps of the scene and helps you to perceive depth and transparencies.

Taj Mahal Illusion

Answer: The mausoleum is the same size in both pictures, though it looks slightly larger in fig. B. This is a real 3D illusion to experiment! In fact, the arch of the main gateway that leads to the famous Taj Mahal induces an interesting optical illusion: if you go to the edge of this arch (fig. A) and walk backwards, the Taj Mahal appears to get bigger (fig. B). Which is in conflict with any perspective rule!

Page 12

Moving Diamonds

Answer: Some regular patterns tend to lose their evenness when assembled in regular sets. The diamond-like shapes have right-angled corners. They also produce a fish-eye lens effect that gives the impression of movement.

Page 12

Rotation Arcs

Answer: The rings are perfectly concentric though they appear to cross over each other. If you move your head the rings will rotate and counter-rotate!

Page 13

Parallel or Connvergent?

Answer: The vertical alignments of colored segments are perfectly parallel to each other.

Page 13

Women Diving

Answer: The upper diver woman appears to be taller than the lower one, despite the fact that both are exactly the same height! Size perception depends strongly on the eye's interpretation of depth cues. Our visual system naturally compensates for size estimations according to perspective: if two objects have the same visual size but one is farther away, the more distant object is felt as larger.

Page 14

Distorted by Fonts?

Answer: Though the upper brown checkered surface appears to shrink towards its center, while the lower one seems to wave, all the squares are perfectly straight and aligned.

Color & Subjective Motion

Page 16

Befuddling Squares

Answer: The blue square A has exactly the same hue as the blue square D (sic!) ... Despite the simultaneous color contrast effect that makes the square A appear brighter than the square D.

Page 16

Unstable Triangles

Answer: Neither, they are exactly the same shade and hue of the triangle-patterned background. Moreover, the Pacman-like shapes give rise to a 3D effect: the triangles seem to slightly hover above the background. This is an interactive variation of the Kanisza triangle illusion.

Page 17

Does Everything Really move?

Answer: You may see large circles or spirals appearing and fading from the radial pattern. This occurs because our visual system is searching to reorganize the zigzags into the best visual interpretation possible.

There is a branch of modern art named Op' Art (short for optic art) that is concerned with visual motion, and uses optical contrasts (such as clear/dark, vertical/horizontal) to induce the illusion of motion in static images, as illustrated by this picture.

Page 17

Kite Pattern

Answer: Line A. The effect that induced you to choose C instead of A is called the "simultaneous brightness contrast" effect.

Page 18

Op' Art Illusion

Answer: Wow! The central blurred red and white strokes seem to move and throb.

Page 18

Magic Spirals?

Answer: The overlapping colored arc segments vividly appear to form spirals, although in reality they are just a series of perfect CONCENTRIC circles (that is circles that share the same center). Moreover, the circles seem to virtually expand and rotate slightly.

Page 19

Puzzling Color

Answer: The tiny balls are actually blue (take a magnifying glass and check it by yourself). The uniform navy blue color of the background and your eyes' movement make them appear green or yellow. Colors are actually altered dramatically by adjacent colors, lightning, and your eye condition. So, under certain conditions, two same colors may appear different, and two different colors may look similar!

Page 20

Color Assimilation

Answer: Yes it is! This vertical alignment of grey bars allows us to discover the effect of "simultaneous color assimilation": it is clearly visible that the color grey of the bars is even on the black background, but when the bars lie on the two-color backgrounds, the portion of the grey bars in contact with another color acquires a similar tone... For instance, the portion of the bar that touches the red color, becomes reddish. This effect gives the overall impression of a color gradation, though the grey is perfectly uniform!

'Color assimilation' effect occurs when some colored elements in a pattern subtend very small angles to the observer, making the color inside those small or thin elements appear to become more like their neighboring colors.

Page 20

Hypno-Discs

Answer: Repeated concentric patterns with contrasted hues cause many people's visual systems to "see" the presence of motion where there is none! If you move your gaze around the picture, the radial patterns will expand while their centers twinkle slightly! The brightness contrast of the patterns and the temporal differences in luminance (brightness) processing produce a signal that tricks our visual motion system.

Page 21

Off-Color Apples

Answer: The colors of the left and right sides of the drawing are restored and will have a perfect balance for 2 up to 5 seconds! This illusion helps to explain why objects look the same color under different lighting environments. This effect is known as "color constancy" or "color adaptation."

Page 21

Blurry Faces

Answer: You will notice that the right image of the woman becomes more blurred than the left one, though they are perfectly identical. The effect only lasts a few seconds. This illusion actually induces a visual after-effect that scientists call 'contrast adaptation' or 'contrast gain control'. This experiment shows that prolonged exposure to unfocused (blurred) images influences visual acuity and contrast sensitivity.

Page 22

Neon Troubles

Answer: The intermittent dark smudges on the three color stripes do not exist. This illusion is caused by a visual mechanism that enhances the contrast of the outline of an object, called "lateral inhibition."

Page 22

Vibrations

Answer: The red grid within the pattern vibrates by intermittence. This is an Op' Art kinetic effect.

Page 23

Hypnosis

Answer: The shading color contrasts will induce a sensation of movement in your brain and the color rings will magically appear to rotate and counter-rotate. The lateral black and white circles too may appear to turn!

Page 23

Oriental Fan

Answer: Yes. The thin dark and bright shades that surround the surfaces give the illusive overall visual impression that they are of two different alternating tones.

Page 24

Unstable Beats

Answer: Obviously not. This is just a kinetic optical illusion. The image is still but the contrasting lines give a slight feeling of motion. The heart also seems to pulsate in rhythm with the observer's breathing.

Page 24

"Eppur Si Muove" (Galileo)

Answer: Though the picture is perfectly still, the black and white contours/shades of the crosses trigger a motion sensation in your peripheral vision. The pattern on the left seems to expand and move toward you, while the pattern on the right appears to recede and shrink.

Page 25

Soccer Ball

Answer: Yes, they are! Only a very few people will guess the right answer, because this illusion is based on the "simultaneous brightness contrast", which is very deceptive due to its powerful illusory effect! Actually, two colored surfaces returning the same amount of light to the eye can look differently bright if the surfaces are – objectively or subjectively – observed in different contexts. Since we rarely see colors in isolation, simultaneous contrast affects our sense of the color that we see.

Page 25

Mycenaean Painting

Answer: The curvilinear shapes of the painted wall are actually all of the same shade! This illusion is related to the "Benussi ring illusion" and is mainly due to the lateral inhibition of our visual system.

Page 26

Ghost Dots?

Answer: There are many explanations and counter-explanations regarding this visual illusion, which is related to the "Hermann grid illusion." The illusory effect disappears if you look at the picture from a distance or too closely.

Page 26

Up and Down Flows

Answer: Yes, it is perfectly still. But sandwiched between the yellow rods, the alignments of purple blurs seem intermittently to brighten and deepen, creating an unending animation of illusory up and down flows.

Page 27

Neon Blue

Answer: Though there is NO blue tint between the blue lines, the curvilinear path appears slightly shaded with blue (the background is actually uniformly white!). This shading effect is called "subjective transparency," "spreading neon color effect", or even "Tron effect."

Page 27

Face of Wonder

Answer: The face will gradually disappear. This is because, viewed with a steady gaze, the slight shade difference between dark and clear colors is a poor stimulus for sustaining visual perception. Eye movement will trigger the reappearance of the face.

Page 28

Pasta Still Life

Answer: The color of the plate is brown (color c) and the decorative circular line is reddish (color 2). The "simultaneous color contrast" makes the colors look very different, indeed!

Page 28

Tunnel Effect

Answer: So weird how the image is static but your eyes can't make the bottom of the tunnel stop expanding forward to you! Wow…

Ambiguous & Impossible Figures

Page 30

Elephant or Bull Delusion Illusion

Answer: The iconic representation of a bull and an elephant fighting and blending their heads together symbolizes the duality of opposites that become one. This kind of images induces a phenomenon of "multistable perception" in the viewer. There are many variants of the illusion in different temples all over India.

Temple of Rameshwaram, Rameshwaram

Temple of Dharasuram, Tamil Nadu

Temple of Birl Mandir, Shahad

Temple of Jalakanteshwara, Vellore

Page 31

Brrr… Scary Night

Answer: The 3-branched candelabrum holds a candle in each arm, but we see only two candles! This candelabrum is an impossible figure based on the infamous "devil's fork," a kind of paradoxical trident with two prongs.

Page 31

Impossible Furniture

Answer: See figs. A and B.

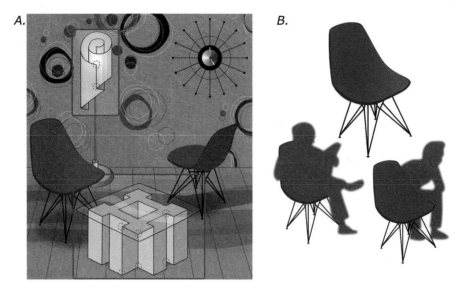

Page 32

Trumpet Player

Answer: Nothing, because it is an unreal, impossible trumpet. Look at the bent brass tubing. It is actually non-continuous tubing! (Maybe that explains the red face of the trumpet player…)

Page 32

Lumberjack

Answer: None of them because they are impossible figures: the higher part of their trunk is not congruent with their respective lower part. In fact, they are shifted one place to the left.

Page 33

Mask of Love?

Answer: Most people who see the picture for the first time do not notice that it is actually both: a woman on the left who kisses a man on the right. Once the viewer discerns two individual faces, his or her brain will 'flip' between two possible interpretations of the mask. This optical illusion was presented to the public by the authors of this book at the 2011 Best Illusion of the Year Contest held at the Philharmonic Center for the Arts in Naples, Florida.

Page 33

Hesitant Bookcase

Answer: Neither of the two… because it is an "impossible figure" that can exist only on paper.

Page 34

Amazing Impossible Structure

Answer: The Y-shaped structures cannot be joined together to form square patterns, unless to intentionally violate the laws of perspective! In real life, the pairs of adjacent sides of such squares wouldn't actually fit together because they would have contrasting perspectives.

Page 34

Enchanted Staircase

Answer: Starting from A and going to the left to cross the bridge the jogger woman will run up and down 14 steps. Starting from A and going to the right, instead, she will climb up and down only 10 steps! This is a tricky optical illusion based on the Penrose staircase: A two-dimensional depiction of a staircase in which the stairs make four 90-degree turns as they ascend or descend, yet form a continuous loop, so that a person could climb them forever and never get any higher.

Page 35

Gift Warp

Answer: This crate is a derivative of Escher's cube. So, it cannot be wrapped because it is an impossible object.

Page 35

Polyvalent Bookshelf

Answer: This is an impossible object. In fact, the books seem magically to face in two contrasting directions.

Page 36

Hallucinatory Staircase

Answer: The kind of staircase you will be tackling here is a novelty in the world of optical illusions. In fact, the architectural structure of the staircase is made in such a way that when a person tries to climb the stairs he or she actually goes down, and vice-versa.

Page 37

Annoying Urban Furniture

Answer: Everyone knows dogs do not like "impossible structures!"

Page 38

Quadri-Dimensional Room?

Answer: The drawing is based on the ambiguous geometric shape called the "Thiéry figure", from the Belgian scientist who devised the illusion. Such a figure appears to exist either above or below the viewer's eye level!

Tests & Experiments

Page 40

Spotting the Blind Spot

Answer: The region where the optic nerve enters the eye is commonly referred to as our "blind spot." This region is in fact blind because it is lacking any photoreceptor cells, that is, cells sensitive to light. So, when light rays reflected from the heart symbol within the playing card fall on your blind spot, it becomes invisible.

Page 40

Honeymoon

Answer: See below.

Page 41

Broken Swiss Cross

Answer: Maybe some of you managed to make a sort of cross like the one illustrated in fig. 1.a... but if you arrange the pieces as shown in fig. 1.b - surprise! - the central empty/blank space outlines a perfect cross. This tricky puzzle belongs to the large family of figure/ground optical illusions. Amazingly, with the pieces of this puzzle you can tessellate an arrangement of octagons (see fig. 2).

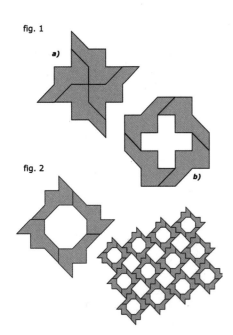

fig. 1

a)

b)

fig. 2

Page 42

Peaceful Scenery?

Answer: An angry man and woman are hidden in the profile of the pedestal (see below). There is also a profile of a little girl outlined by the trunk and the foliage of the bonsai.

This type of illusion is related to the "Rubin's vase" illusion, named after the Danish psychologist Edgar Rubin. He introduced it in his work, *Synsoplevede Figurer* (Visual Figures), published around 1915. Nevertheless, Rubin did NOT discover the Rubin's vase illusion! The illustration and the wooden turned urns respectively in figs. A and B, date back to the French revolution and show probably the earliest Rubin's vase-like illusions. You can see, in effect, the profiles of Louis XVI and his family outlined by the contour of various urns and trees.

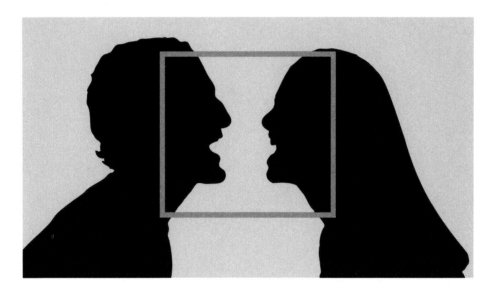

A.

B.

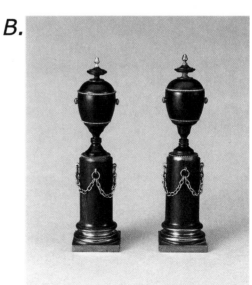

Page 43

St. Patrick Visual Puzzle

Answer: The 5 four-leaf clovers are in 3B, 7B, 5C, 1D, and 7/8D.

Page 43

Ambiguous Message

Answer: The hidden message is "love." To transform "hate" into "love," place the image in front of a mirror as shown.

Page 44

Wow effect

Answer: After a short time, you will have the sensation that what you are walking beneath is actually right in front of you!

Looking in the mirror, you may actually see a virtual surrounding and will experience two major illusive sensations:
1. Walking through solid matter when "an object" stands in "front of you."
2. Levitating into thin air if there is a "hole" in "front of you."

Page 45

Crack the Message

Answer: The message reads: "This message serves to prove how our mind can do amazing things! Impressive things! In the beginning it was hard but now on this line your mind is reading it automatically without even thinking about it!". This experiment shows how our minds can interpret certain things that look like words, even if they aren't spelled correctly, are jumbled slightly, or in this specific case, have some letters turned into numbers.

Page 46

The Unsizable Square

Answer: 80% of people answer diamond B, but the correct answer is actually diamond A!

Page 46

Mystery Comb

Answer: Someone is hidden within the alignment of black spikes. Can you guess who? Elvis Presley! — Look at the picture from a distance.

Page 47

Halloween Popcorn

Answer: 7 at least! See the picture below.

Page 47

Crack this Martian Sentence

Answer: The sentence reads: "Blank spaces are actually letters." This is what linguists call a self-referential sentence!

Page 48

Young Girl with Cat

Answer: No, your eyes aren't going funny, the cat has really 4 eyes! What is interesting about double-eyed illusions, is that people have trouble seeing them. What makes your eyes dizzy is the fact they are trying to focus while your brain is fighting to give you the most coherent image of a cat.

Page 49

Hidden Zebras

Answer: See picture below.

Page 49

Camouflaged?

Answer: No, of course. This simple yet effective illusion is based on specular reflections.

Page 50

Hidden Giraffe

Answer: Look at his neck!

Page 51

Pair of Oddness

Answer: The bottle is concealed between the two glasses. The other oddity is that it is impossible to say if the candlestick has two or three sticks.

Page 51

Mysterious Reflection

Answer: It isn't actually a mirror. The shadows wouldn't be like shown in the picture (both should approach the supposed mirror). Hence, what we simply have is a vase with flowers facing a vase without flowers, and a glass plate in between them.

Page 52

Haunted House

Answer: A ghostly face can be seen between the two dogs on the pathway.

Page 53

Incomplete Keyboard

Answer: Actually, the sentence contains all the letters of the alphabet. Maybe you have answered that the letter 'F' is missing... this is because you couldn't find it in the word 'of'. Function words like 'of', 'from', 'and' are unconsciously processed by your brain as they haven't any specific lexical meaning for the text.

Page 53

Batches

Answer: If you discard batch number 2, exactly five distinct sets of clocks will be left.

Page 54

Hidden Portrait

Answer: Close up this picture makes no sense, but if you see it from a distance you will perceive the portrait of Mona Lisa, the most famous Leonardo Da Vinci painting. This serves to demonstrate the remarkable ability of our brains in recognizing faces, even when they are obscured in one way or another.